THE JOURNAL

www.PauseStopReset.com

This Journal belongs to

It was started on

The Journal and its contents are private property and strictly confidential.
If found, please return to its rightful owner:

Call

Email

For information on how to use the journal
and frequently asked questions please go to
portal.pausestopreset.com/journal-faqs

Infinite thanks to Terry x

Welcome To The Journal

The first thing to know is there are no rules as to how you use this journal. Yes really it's yours to use as you choose. We have some suggestions and it's a tool to help you and a safe space for you to note, observe and more.

It's also a work in progress, as I am and I believe everything is.

So much of modern advice and ideas is about planning and building habits, structures and systems in order to make something happen or avoid something else.

Yes that can be useful, and we've mastered and developed many of them over the decades. However I realised there was something else that seemed to live in those magical moments, when things just work out beyond your dreams or when things aren't working and you need a miracle.

You see my goal is for you always to be right here and now fully present to who you truly are, and in that space and state be able to focus on and prioritise what you choose to – optimally.

Human Beings are called that for a reason - not human Doings or Havings.

You'll be amazed at what's possible to cause, create, experience and more as you **Pause Stop Reset**, and more importantly at who you can become.

So ready to explore what's possible ?

With love now and always,

Simon Hedley | Strategic Alchemist
SimonHedley.com

How do you use The Journal?

The journal is your tool to use as you think fit, and as fits you. How you use it will most likely change and develop over time as you use it more. Do celebrate the fact that you are using it. The journal is a gift that you give to yourself and the world each time you use it to help you **Pause Stop Reset**. My intention is that you enjoy exploring how you can use it with more joy and benefits. To get you started here are some of the pages within the journal and a quick start guide on how you can use them.

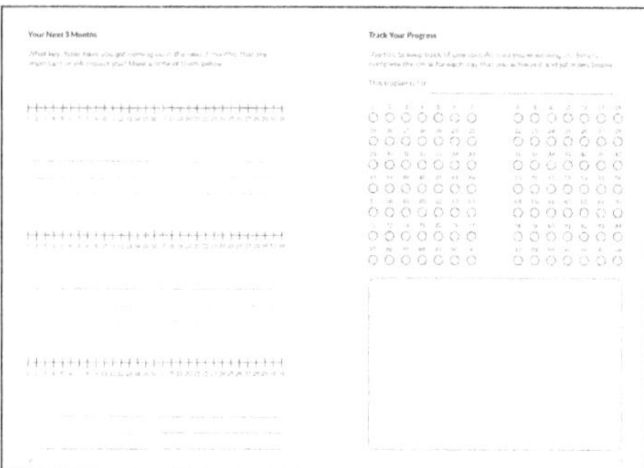

Your Next 3 Months

Highlight key dates already set in your calendar or think about the next 3 months. This is a master technique; a great way to give yourself a north star to come back to and revisit to have a clear bigger picture focus. Remember less is more... less is so much more.

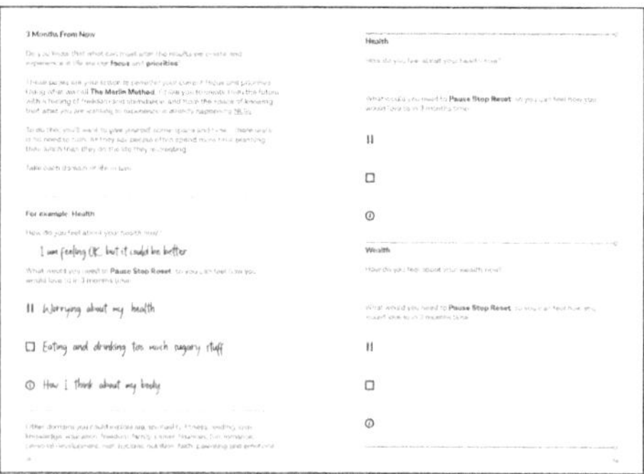

Three Months From Now

Consider different areas of your life. There is space to journal the ways you can see you could choose to **Pause Stop Reset** and which will help you move towards your goals. We've given you some common frames and also space to create your own.

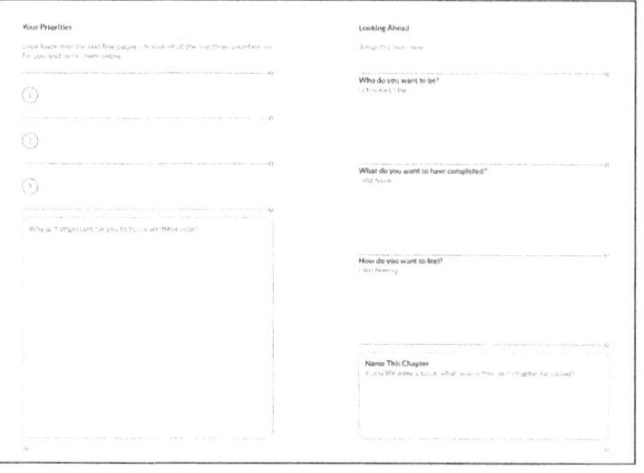

Your Priorities

Having focus and a place to track progress is powerful. Choose your priorities and then track how you do. This section is all about helping you visualise and internalise your goals, so you're best able to achieve them.

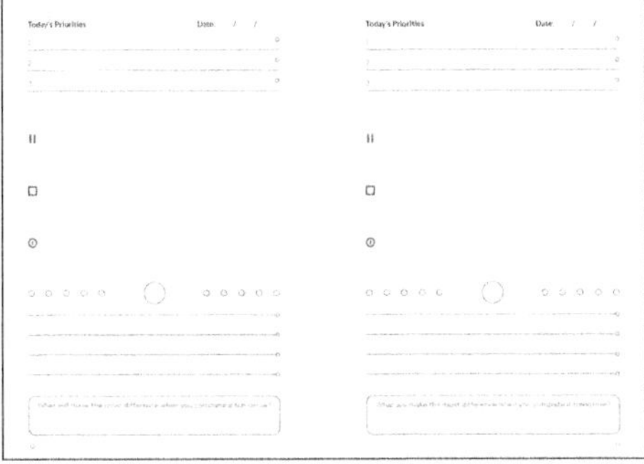

Daily Journal Page

The Daily Journal Page is where you have the structure to create and capture your daily insights, observations and progress.

This is the heart of the journal, and a resource I hope you'll always have to hand.

Invest at least 5 minutes each morning in yourself and choose your day's priorities. Personally, I recommend you also use the app **i-Prioritize.com**, this can help you really focus on your choice of priorities.

You then have space during the day as needed or when you pause to check in to note down areas where you did, wish you had, or could have used **Pause Stop Reset**. At the end of the day or during a regular scheduled time we recommend you review your progress and record that.

There is a grid structure that you can flex to your taste. Have fun and feel into what works for you. Remember this is your journal – colour, fun and creativity is allowed and encouraged. There is then space for observations. I like to record things I'm genuinely grateful for, insights, people that made a difference, the big wow moments. Then there is the key question to think about and note before you go to sleep.

The large circle for example can be used in many ways, for example:

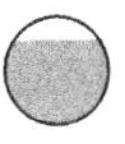

Questions to journal on

You can add your own and build a resource to consider and meditate on. Sometimes the most powerful thing is to focus on the Key Question that has you consider things from a different perspective. Learn more at **www.TheKeyQuestions.com**

Pause

Stop

Reset

Three little words that make the difference.

There, we've started now, and in this introduction I'm going to share a little about what these three words are and why they are so capable of making such a difference.

The first thing is to take note of them, whether that's a mental note or a written one in a journal, a photo or a social media post.

The three symbols are a reminder of the three little words **Pause Stop Reset**, and from now on you're going to start noticing and seeing them more and more in the world.

When you do, then remember these three little words:
Pause Stop Reset.

Why are these words important?

I'd ask you to trust me, and I also don't think that's the most useful answer.

I can tell you with my hand on my heart that these three little words - **Pause Stop Reset**™ - have made and continue to make all the difference to me.

My greatest wish is that I had learnt them earlier, and that I would have committed to mastering them earlier as well in different ways.

Even to this today I'm still a beginner student in so many ways, learning how they can be applied consistently and in new ways, and yet I've noticed how they give me options and an experience in relationships and in life I never really knew was possible.

I've seen how countless friends, students and clients time and time again get stuck and have no capacity or awareness that they really do have the choice to **Pause Stop Reset**™ until I start to share it with them and provide them with an actual space and experience to relearn what these words mean and how to apply the distinctions in reality.

The sad truth and expensive lessons for myself have been that when I most needed them, I didn't know them (or had forgotten); either way, when it mattered I didn't have them mastered, let alone have the ability to use them optimally.

In a simple practical sense, the day when I was driving back in the early evening and a car ahead of me suddenly put on its brakes, and as I tried to do an emergency stop, the brakes in my car failed and my car struck the "wall" and became written off, and I was left wondering what just happened.

In that moment I knew I wanted to stop. I pressed the brake to stop. I did what I had been taught to do. However, it didn't work at all. The car did not stop. I did not stop. The mechanics weren't there; it turned out the brake line had failed even though the car had just passed its MOT. So there I was, despite having the tool and training, I hadn't been able to stop when I most needed to. In life we don't get the instructions, certification and MOT for the things that matter. Yes, lots of options to learn – and yet, how often have you said something in the moment you later regret? Or eaten something while thinking or saying, "I really shouldn't"?

It still fascinates me that we live in a world where we can so easily create sub-optimal results and that if only we could **Pause Stop Reset**, we could navigate it so much more elegantly and effectively.

To ground out the costs of not knowing and applying Pause Stop Reset, the result is countless moments of wasted time, money and opportunities; lost relationships that didn't need to end up the way they did; and the biggest challenge of regret.

Over time this builds.

The good news is that the reset can start today, and in this moment, everything can change. And it begins not on the outside but on the inner, and doesn't depend on any education, financial or other resources.

Wherever you are, you can remember these three little words.

Pause Stop Reset.

May you always
choose to breathe,
smile and take the
journey, one step
at a time.

Your Next 3 Months

What key dates have you got coming up in the next 3 months, that are important or will impact you? Make a note of them below.

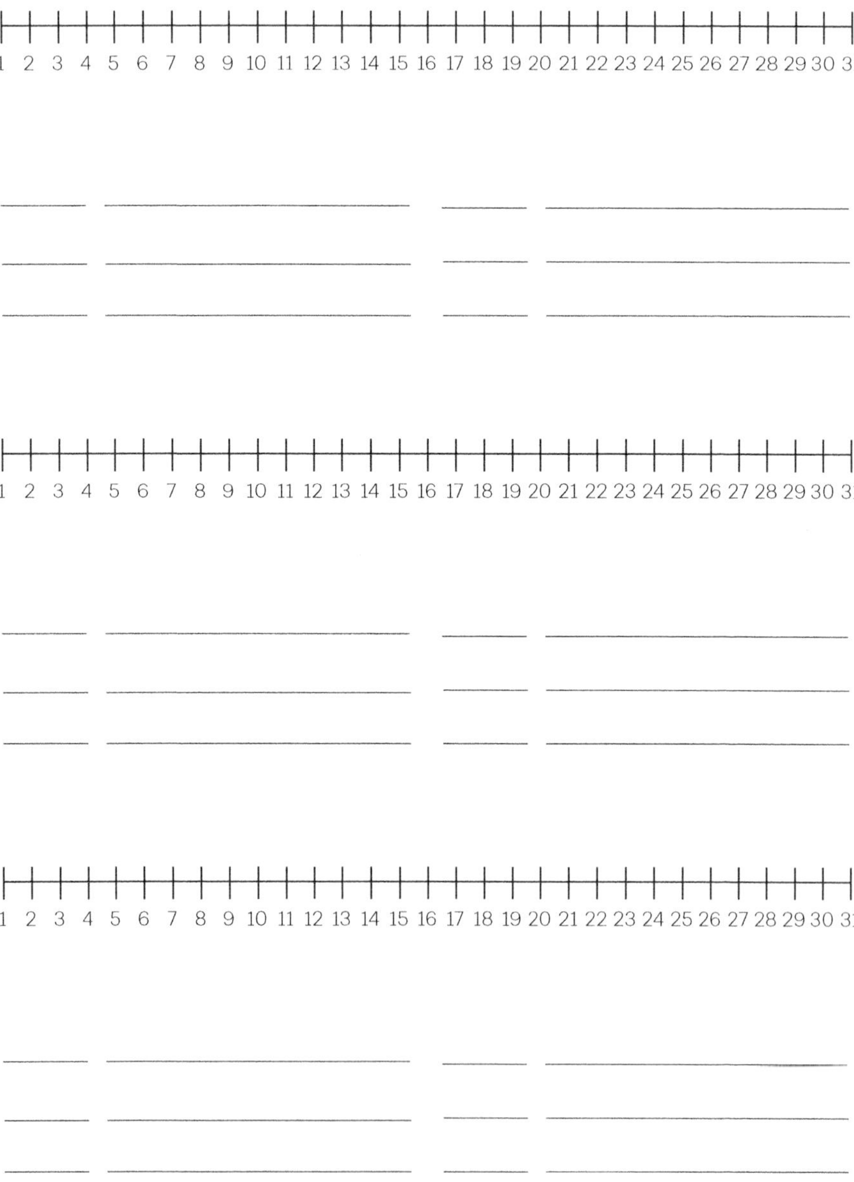

Track Your Progress

Use this to keep track of one specific area you're working on. Simply complete the circle for each day that you achieve it and jot notes below.

This tracker is for: ______________________

1	2	3	4	5	6	7	8	9	10	11	12	13	14
○	○	○	○	○	○	○	○	○	○	○	○	○	○
15	16	17	18	19	20	21	22	23	24	25	26	27	28
○	○	○	○	○	○	○	○	○	○	○	○	○	○
29	30	31	32	33	34	35	36	37	38	39	40	41	42
○	○	○	○	○	○	○	○	○	○	○	○	○	○
43	44	45	46	47	48	49	50	51	52	53	54	55	56
○	○	○	○	○	○	○	○	○	○	○	○	○	○
57	58	59	60	61	62	63	64	65	66	67	68	69	70
○	○	○	○	○	○	○	○	○	○	○	○	○	○
71	72	73	74	75	76	77	78	79	80	81	82	83	84
○	○	○	○	○	○	○	○	○	○	○	○	○	○
85	86	87	88	89	90	91	92	93	94	95	96	97	98
○	○	○	○	○	○	○	○	○	○	○	○	○	○

3 Months From Now

Do you know that what can most alter the results we create and experience in life are our **focus** and **priorities**?

These pages are your space to consider your current focus and priorities. Using what we call **The Merlin Method**, I'd like you to create from the future with a feeling of freedom and abundance, and from the space of knowing that what you are wanting to experience is already happening NOW.

To do this, you'll want to give yourself some space and time - there really is no need to rush. As they say people often spend more time planning their lunch than they do the life they're creating.

Take each domain of life in turn.

For example: Health

How do you feel about your health now?

I am feeling OK, but it could be better

What would you need to **Pause Stop Reset**, so you can feel how you would love to in 3 months time:

II Worrying about my health

☐ Eating and drinking too much sugary stuff

⏻ How I think about my body

Other domains you could explore are; spirituality, fitness, reading, love, knowledge, education, freedom, family, career, finances, fun, romance, personal development, rest, hobbies, nutrition, faith, parenting and emotions.

Health

How do you feel about your health now?

What would you need to **Pause Stop Reset**, so you can feel how you would love to in 3 months time:

II

☐

⏻

Wealth

How do you feel about your wealth now?

What would you need to **Pause Stop Reset**, so you can feel how you would love to in 3 months time:

II

☐

⏻

Wisdom

How do you feel about your wisdom now?

What would you need to **Pause Stop Reset**, so you can feel how you would love to in 3 months time:

Relationships

How do you feel about your relationships now?

What would you need to **Pause Stop Reset**, so you can feel how you would love to in 3 months time:

Personal Life

How do you feel about your personal life now?

What would you need to **Pause Stop Reset**, so you can feel how you would love to in 3 months time:

Legacy

How do you feel about your legacy now?

What would you need to **Pause Stop Reset**, so you can feel how you would love to in 3 months time:

How do you feel about this now?

What would you need to **Pause Stop Reset**, so you can feel how you would love to in 3 months time:

II

☐

⏻

How do you feel about this now?

What would you need to **Pause Stop Reset**, so you can feel how you would love to in 3 months time:

II

☐

⏻

Your Priorities

Look back over the last few pages, choose what the top three priorities are for you and write them below.

1

2

3

Why is it important for you to focus on these now?

Looking Ahead

3 months from now...

Who do you want to be?
I choose to be...

What do you want to have completed?
I will have...

How do you want to feel?
I am feeling...

Name This Chapter
If you life were a book, what would this next chapter be called?

Remember always that
neither this moment,
nor my past,
need to define me
or the future.

Today's Priorities **Date: / /**

1.

2.

3.

What will make the most difference when you complete it tomorrow?

Today's Priorities **Date: / /**

1.

2.

3.

What will make the most difference when you complete it tomorrow?

Today's Priorities **Date: / /**

1.

2.

3.

What will make the most difference when you complete it tomorrow?

Today's Priorities **Date: / /**

1.

2.

3.

What will make the most difference when you complete it tomorrow?

Today's Priorities **Date: / /**

1.

2.

3.

What will make the most difference when you complete it tomorrow?

Today's Priorities **Date: / /**

1.

2.

3.

What will make the most difference when you complete it tomorrow?

Today's Priorities **Date: / /**

1.

2.

3.

What will make the most difference when you complete it tomorrow?

People massively
underestimate
who they are today
and who they can
become in a decade.

Today's Priorities **Date: / /**

1.

2.

3.

What will make the most difference when you complete it tomorrow?

Today's Priorities **Date: / /**

1.

2.

3.

What will make the most difference when you complete it tomorrow?

Today's Priorities **Date: / /**

1.

2.

3.

What will make the most difference when you complete it tomorrow?

Today's Priorities Date: / /

1.

2.

3.

What will make the most difference when you complete it tomorrow?

Today's Priorities Date: / /

1.

2.

3.

What will make the most difference when you complete it tomorrow?

Today's Priorities **Date: / /**

1.

2.

3.

What will make the most difference when you complete it tomorrow?

Today's Priorities **Date:** / /

1. ○

2. ○

3. ○

What will make the most difference when you complete it tomorrow?

Maybe, I guess,
the universe knows
whats best for all of us...

And perhaps,
on the good days,
we remember and agree.

Today's Priorities **Date: / /**

1.
2.
3.

What will make the most difference when you complete it tomorrow?

Today's Priorities **Date: / /**

1.

2.

3.

What will make the most difference when you complete it tomorrow?

Today's Priorities **Date: / /**

1. ○

2. ○

3. ○

What will make the most difference when you complete it tomorrow?

Today's Priorities **Date: / /**

1.

2.

3.

What will make the most difference when you complete it tomorrow?

Today's Priorities **Date: / /**

1. ○
2. ○
3. ○

○

○

○

○

What will make the most difference when you complete it tomorrow?

Today's Priorities **Date: / /**

1.

2.

3.

What will make the most difference when you complete it tomorrow?

Today's Priorities **Date: / /**

1.

2.

3.

What will make the most difference when you complete it tomorrow?

You can wait
to be chosen.

Or you can choose
your quest and path.

S.p

Today's Priorities **Date: / /**

1.

2.

3.

What will make the most difference when you complete it tomorrow?

Today's Priorities **Date: / /**

1.

2.

3.

What will make the most difference when you complete it tomorrow?

Today's Priorities **Date: / /**

1.

2.

3.

What will make the most difference when you complete it tomorrow?

Today's Priorities **Date: / /**

1.

2.

3.

What will make the most difference when you complete it tomorrow?

Today's Priorities **Date: / /**

1.

2.

3.

What will make the most difference when you complete it tomorrow?

Today's Priorities **Date: / /**

1.

2.

3.

What will make the most difference when you complete it tomorrow?

Today's Priorities **Date: / /**

1. ○

2. ○

3. ○

○ ○ ○ ○ ○ ○ ○ ○ ○ ○ ○

What will make the most difference when you complete it tomorrow?

Onwards;

one breath

at a time.

Today's Priorities **Date: / /**

1.

2.

3.

What will make the most difference when you complete it tomorrow?

Today's Priorities **Date: / /**

1.

2.

3.

What will make the most difference when you complete it tomorrow?

Today's Priorities **Date: / /**

1.

2.

3.

What will make the most difference when you complete it tomorrow?

Today's Priorities **Date: / /**

1.

2.

3.

What will make the most difference when you complete it tomorrow?

Today's Priorities **Date: / /**

1.

2.

3.

What will make the most difference when you complete it tomorrow?

Today's Priorities **Date: / /**

1.

2.

3.

What will make the most difference when you complete it tomorrow?

Today's Priorities **Date: / /**

1.

2.

3.

What will make the most difference when you complete it tomorrow?

You are,
and always were,
more than enough.

Today's Priorities **Date: / /**

1.

2.

3.

What will make the most difference when you complete it tomorrow?

Today's Priorities **Date: / /**

1.

2.

3.

What will make the most difference when you complete it tomorrow?

Today's Priorities **Date: / /**

1.

2.

3.

What will make the most difference when you complete it tomorrow?

Today's Priorities

Date: / /

1.
2.
3.

What will make the most difference when you complete it tomorrow?

Today's Priorities **Date: / /**

1.

2.

3.

What will make the most difference when you complete it tomorrow?

Today's Priorities Date: / /

1.

2.

3.

What will make the most difference when you complete it tomorrow?

Today's Priorities **Date: / /**

1.

2.

3.

What will make the most difference when you complete it tomorrow?

Be grateful
for the big things
and the small things.

Today's Priorities **Date: / /**

1. ○
2. ○
3. ○

○ ○ ○ ○ ○ ◯ ○ ○ ○ ○ ○

What will make the most difference when you complete it tomorrow?

Today's Priorities **Date: / /**

1.

2.

3.

What will make the most difference when you complete it tomorrow?

Today's Priorities **Date: / /**

1.

2.

3.

What will make the most difference when you complete it tomorrow?

Today's Priorities **Date: / /**

1.

2.

3.

What will make the most difference when you complete it tomorrow?

Today's Priorities **Date: / /**

1.

2.

3.

What will make the most difference when you complete it tomorrow?

Today's Priorities **Date: / /**

1.

2.

3.

What will make the most difference when you complete it tomorrow?

Today's Priorities **Date: / /**

1.

2.

3.

What will make the most difference when you complete it tomorrow?

Choose the life
you want to live.

Today's Priorities **Date: / /**

1.

2.

3.

What will make the most difference when you complete it tomorrow?

Today's Priorities **Date: / /**

1.

2.

3.

What will make the most difference when you complete it tomorrow?

Today's Priorities **Date: / /**

1.

2.

3.

What will make the most difference when you complete it tomorrow?

Today's Priorities **Date: / /**

1.

2.

3.

What will make the most difference when you complete it tomorrow?

Today's Priorities **Date: / /**

1.

2.

3.

What will make the most difference when you complete it tomorrow?

Today's Priorities **Date: / /**

1.

2.

3.

What will make the most difference when you complete it tomorrow?

Today's Priorities **Date: / /**

1. ○

2. ○

3. ○

○ ○ ○ ○ ○ ◯ ○ ○ ○ ○ ○

What will make the most difference when you complete it tomorrow?

You are

incredible.

Today's Priorities **Date: / /**

1.

2.

3.

What will make the most difference when you complete it tomorrow?

Today's Priorities **Date: / /**

1.

2.

3.

What will make the most difference when you complete it tomorrow?

Today's Priorities **Date: / /**

1.

2.

3.

What will make the most difference when you complete it tomorrow?

Today's Priorities **Date: / /**

1.

2.

3.

What will make the most difference when you complete it tomorrow?

Today's Priorities **Date: / /**

1.

2.

3.

What will make the most difference when you complete it tomorrow?

Today's Priorities **Date: / /**

1.

2.

3.

What will make the most difference when you complete it tomorrow?

Today's Priorities **Date: / /**

1.
2.
3.

What will make the most difference when you complete it tomorrow?

When you don't think you can pause is often when you most need to.

Today's Priorities **Date: / /**

1.

2.

3.

What will make the most difference when you complete it tomorrow?

Today's Priorities **Date: / /**

1.

2.

3.

What will make the most difference when you complete it tomorrow?

Today's Priorities **Date:** / /

1. ○

2. ○

3. ○

What will make the most difference when you complete it tomorrow?

Today's Priorities **Date: / /**

1.

2.

3.

What will make the most difference when you complete it tomorrow?

Today's Priorities **Date: / /**

1.

2.

3.

What will make the most difference when you complete it tomorrow?

Today's Priorities **Date: / /**

1.

2.

3.

What will make the most difference when you complete it tomorrow?

Today's Priorities **Date: / /**

1. ○

2. ○

3. ○

What will make the most difference when you complete it tomorrow?

When you
Pause Stop Reset
you give the universe a
chance to catch up
and realign with your
infinite intelligence.

Today's Priorities **Date: / /**

1. ○

2. ○

3. ○

What will make the most difference when you complete it tomorrow?

Today's Priorities **Date: / /**

1.

2.

3.

What will make the most difference when you complete it tomorrow?

Today's Priorities **Date: / /**

1.

2.

3.

What will make the most difference when you complete it tomorrow?

Today's Priorities **Date: / /**

1.

2.

3.

What will make the most difference when you complete it tomorrow?

Today's Priorities **Date: / /**

1.

2.

3.

What will make the most difference when you complete it tomorrow?

Today's Priorities **Date: / /**

1. ○

2. ○

3. ○

○ ○ ○ ○ ○ ○ ○ ○ ○ ○ ○

What will make the most difference when you complete it tomorrow?

Today's Priorities **Date: / /**

1.

2.

3.

What will make the most difference when you complete it tomorrow?

When we speak
it's easy to forget
to listen and think.

Today's Priorities **Date: / /**

1.

2.

3.

What will make the most difference when you complete it tomorrow?

Today's Priorities **Date: / /**

1.

2.

3.

What will make the most difference when you complete it tomorrow?

Today's Priorities **Date: / /**

1.

2.

3.

What will make the most difference when you complete it tomorrow?

Today's Priorities **Date: / /**

1.

2.

3.

What will make the most difference when you complete it tomorrow?

Today's Priorities **Date: / /**

1.

2.

3.

What will make the most difference when you complete it tomorrow?

Today's Priorities **Date: / /**

1.

2.

3.

What will make the most difference when you complete it tomorrow?

Today's Priorities **Date: / /**

1.

2.

3.

What will make the most difference when you complete it tomorrow?

Remember the
greatest orchards
sometimes started
with a single seed.

Today's Priorities **Date: / /**

1.

2.

3.

What will make the most difference when you complete it tomorrow?

Today's Priorities **Date: / /**

1.

2.

3.

What will make the most difference when you complete it tomorrow?

Today's Priorities **Date: / /**

1. ○
2. ○
3. ○

What will make the most difference when you complete it tomorrow?

Today's Priorities **Date: / /**

1.

2.

3.

What will make the most difference when you complete it tomorrow?

Today's Priorities **Date: / /**

1.

2.

3.

What will make the most difference when you complete it tomorrow?

Today's Priorities **Date: / /**

1.

2.

3.

What will make the most difference when you complete it tomorrow?

Today's Priorities **Date: / /**

1. ○

2. ○

3. ○

○ ○ ○ ○ ○ ○ ○ ○ ○ ○ ○

What will make the most difference when you complete it tomorrow?

Will you live a life
you truly love,
or will you keep wishing
you didn't
know you could?

S.p

My biggest lessons

When you reflect on the last three months, what are the biggest lessons you learned or things you'll take with you?

I am thankful for

When you reflect on the last three months, what are the top three things you are most grateful for?

My best memories

When you reflect on the last three months, what are your favourite three memories of this time?

People that mattered

When you reflect on the last three months, who were the top three people that impacted you (good or bad) and why?

With hindsight

If you could go back in time, what would you have...

Paused

Stopped

Reset

Name This Chapter

Looking back over the last 3 months, what would you name this chapter?

Looking forward

What will you be taking forward into your next 3 months?

II ☐ ⓘ

Inside each person,
including you now, is the
potential for almost
infinite creativity
and more than you
could ever imagine.

S.P.

The Key Questions

Journalling is a powerful tool and below are some key questions that you can explore when you choose to spend some time reflecting. I've also left space for you to add your own. Whether you write on these or think about them, they'll still give you clarity that you can use to make positive changes and choices. Discover more at **www.TheKeyQuestions.com**

What question are you asking yourself this week?

o How is this helping you?

What 3 things are you most grateful for right now?

What do you most need to learn now?

Who would you most love to speak with now?

Who could you add most value to right now?

What would you love to experience now?

II ☐ ⓘ

P.S. It occurs to me
there is another option,
perhaps you don't
have to be a
"lord of the universe",
often it seems that it is more
than enough for you to just
simply be yourself.

S.p.

First published in Great Britain 2020
The Simple Idea Ltd

Artwork, Design and layout: Sophie, Rachel, Joe and Si
www.AuthorMarketingGroup.com

If you've enjoyed this journal, you may well enjoy other books, guides, resources and more from **The Simple Idea**™ which you can find out about at **Shop.TheSimpleIdea.com**

Discover **Pause Stop Reset** bonuses at **portal.pausestopreset.com/journal-bonus** (or scan the above QR code)

Simon Hedley | Strategic Alchemist

Known by his clients, partners and friends as **The Strategic Alchemist™**, Simon has been the secret weapon of many well-known leaders and founders for over two decades.

He qualified as a Chartered Accountant with PwC where he identified a major global fraud and went on to work in finance & banking with a focus on structuring and investment management.

He's provided strategic advisory services to Founders, Entrepreneurs and Investors for over two decades, often acting as an authenticator and connector.

Simon is the author of several books including **Pause Stop Reset™**.

Discover the latest **Pause Stop Reset™** updates and opportunities at **www.PauseStopReset.com**

Learn more about Simon at **www.SimonHedley.com**

Printed in Great Britain
by Amazon

70364759R00108